Face Time

My Encounter with Him

#1 International Best Selling Author Alisa Tyler

Heart Centered Women Publishing™

Charleston, South Carolina

ISBN-13: 978-1976488689

ISBN-10: 1976488680

Published and distributed in the United States by: Heart Centered Women Publishing™ www.heartcenteredwomenpublishing.com

Published and distributed Internationally by: Heart Centered Women Publishing™ www.heartcenteredwomenpublishing.com

Cover Design by: Nobles Darby, IV www.elavatemarketing.com

Interior Design by: Heart Centered Women Publishing™ www.heartcenteredwomenpublishing.com

Acknowledgements

First, I would like to give glory and honor to my Lord and savior Jesus Christ for your grace and mercy. Thank you Lord for birthing this story, at the time I was experiencing it I didn't understand the bigger picture you had for my life. Thank you for taking my broken pieces and putting them back together again. Without you I would be nothing. You are my joy, my peace, my hope, my everything. May you get all the glory out of this project.

I would like to express my gratitude to the many people who saw me through this book; to all those who provided support, talked things over, read, offered comments, assisted in the editing, proofreading and design. Specials thanks to Natasha Brown for assisting me with my content and helping me to express my story the way it was given to me.

Special thanks to Heart Centered Women Publishing™ for giving me the opportunity to share my story. Charlotte, I truly appreciate your patience and continued words of encouragement throughout this process. May the Lord continue to bless you and your company for having a heart to open a platform where women can share their stories.

Thank you, Nobles Darby IV, CEO of Elavate Marketing for your creativity and marketing skills and for designing my book cover, logo, and website.

Elder Mark Jackson, special thanks for being such an awesome Worship leader and for taking time out of your busy schedule to write my Foreword. It truly meant a lot.

I would like to thank Herb Bias Photography for the professional photos for my book cover. Suellen ElleDiva Brown Owner of The Glam-Her Crown for a fabulous job on my makeup. Joshena AKA J.J. Owner of "The Wow Factor" salon for being an awesome hair stylist. Stephano owner of Stephano & Co Salon for providing an atmosphere of excellence and giving my hair a polished finish for my website photos. Chris Da'Shawn Harris thanks for providing your photography services on location.

My loving parents Emanuel & May Della Riley who have always supported me and encouraged me to finish my book. Your prayers and unconditional love has truly brought me through everything. Dad thanks for pushing me to focus on completing my book, instead of trying to figure out where the resources would come from to get it complete. You said God would send them, and he did.

To my daughter Ashley, you are so innovative and creative and have such a natural gift for expressing yourself. Thanks for your ideas. My beautiful grandchildren Jordyn, Jeremiah and Aaliyah everything I do is to leave a legacy for you.

To my Pastor Dr. RA Vernon of The Word Church for being such a great example of never give up and always continue to pursue your goals. You always say 2-5 years is coming anyway, if not now when will you pursue your destiny. Lady Victory Vernon thanks for all your Chatroom/Women's Wednesday sessions that changed my life, and motivated me to pursue my destiny.

I want to thank Apostle Phyllis Carter one of my spiritual mentors for coming into my life and standing in the gap and speaking into my life through your Journey to the Well teachings at Messiah International Ministries.

To all my many friends who supported me during my journey. Whether it was a text, visit, monetary contribution, or prayer it was greatly appreciated. All my prayer warrior intercessors thanks for standing in the gap for me, times when I wanted to give up I know it was your consistent prayers that brought me through.

Finally, I want to thank YOU for purchasing *Face Time.*

I pray my book inspires you to never give up on your dreams. I always say delayed but never forgotten. I hope it provokes you to evaluate your *Face Time* with God and if you have allowed distractions to interfere with your Face Time as I did, that you will seek the Lord and allow him to show you the plan he has for your life.

Last, that you remember who you are, you were wonderfully handcrafted by God to be someone's answer, not from degrees but from your life experiences. Nothing happened to you by chance, it was all ordained by the will of God so you could be exactly where you are today. You were created for a purpose and as you pursue your purpose it will provide provision.

No matter where you came from or what you may still be going through, you are destined for greatness, so keep it moving. I pray the content of *Face Time* blesses you and provokes you to act today because no day is promised to any of us.

With Love,

Alisa Tyler

Foreword by Elder Mark T. Jackson

I must admit, there have been countless days of my life where I have allowed the busyness of my schedule, the desire to strive toward financial increase and debt elimination, the mandates of educational pursuit, or just spending leisure time with family and friends to trump spending quality time with God. If you are not intentional to spend daily quality time with God, you could easily find yourself more irritable, making poor decisions, attracting unnecessary drama to your life.

God desires to meet with us daily and for us to value His presence more than anything else in the world. The first command given to Moses in Exodus Chapter 20, verse 3 was "You shall have no other gods before me." We can so easily put our mate, our children, our education, our business, our health, our ministry, recreation, social media, and so much more before Him. Anything that we put before Him becomes and idol.

Alisa Tyler ignites a passion in every believer and triggers a flame in every unbeliever to consider spending *Face Time* with God. She transparently details her life experiences and shares how Face Time with God anchored her and guided her through the most challenging seasons of her life.

Whether you are a single mother challenged to take care of your children without the aid of a significant other, in pursuit of higher education, fighting toward financial stability, recovering from a discombobulating divorce, or simply believing for the supernatural to transpire in your life, this book will encourage you and become a seed in the soil of your success. Your future can be fantastic or traumatic pending on the amount of *Face Time* you share with God.

Alisa Tyler raises the argument and posits that our society is vastly drifting into a technologically savvy society and has replaced *Face Time* with God with gadgets, television, online surfing, and social media mediums. She illuminates the fact that we have become desensitized to the Kingdom agenda and challenges us to return to prayer and spending time face to face with God. If anyone can beckon us back to this place of intimacy with God, it is Alisa.

I was granted the esteemed privilege to share in ministry with Alisa as her ministry leader. She served faithfully on the praise team for years until her bat with illness. Many people would have given up and thrown in the towel. Alisa held on to her faith and continued attending worship services, serving wherever she could serve.

She never seemed to have anything negative to say. She was optimistic and stood on the fact that God could heal and deliver her. She was relentless in her pursuit and fully persuaded that God would indeed heal her and she would be back on her feet. She has looked death in the face. She has sojourned through the storm. She has documented her *Face Time* with Death vice versa *Face Time* with God and has lived to tell the story.

As you read this book, I admonish you to take down your defense and be receptive to the wisdom that will be released to you. I have been so blessed and so challenged after reading this book to heighten my *Face Time* with God and have been made aware of the countless benefits of doing so. I admonish you to take this journey as well. God wants more *Face Time* with you.

Elder Mark T. Jackson

Table of Contents

Chapter 1

Spending Face Time with God

"Like Wi-Fi on our cellphones, when you're not in a service area that transmits God, you can't pick up His signal."

Fast forward to the beginning of the end—CODE BLUE....

I couldn't walk. I couldn't talk. Breathing through my nose and mouth seemed like the hardest feat ever. These symptoms let me know that I couldn't wait any longer. I rushed to the hospital to face my fate. My blood pressure was rapidly increasing and the doctors and nurses rushed to strap me onto a bed and plug in the oxygen machines. The beeping, the scurry, the voices around me were controlled, yet urgent—it was just like a dramatic hospital sitcom, or movie, only this was real, and it was me who was the cause of concern. Is this the beginning of the end? I thought. As the possibility of death began to invade my thoughts and as my imagination took a wrong turn toward defeat, God stepped in, and declared, "Not so. This is my daughter who I ordained to LIVE and proclaim the gospel for my glory.

How often do we ever think to stop and have *Face Time* with God? Today, cell phones, iPads, and television have replaced much-needed time with the Father that we all so desperately need.

Unless you're reading the Bible app on your mobile device, you cannot find God on a telephone or tablet. An encounter with God is only established through face-to-face contact. The Lord spoke to Moses face-to-face, as a man speaks to his friend. Exodus 33:1 (NIV) No doubt an encounter with God may be much different than the burning bush experience that Moses had.

Yet you have something that Moses did not have – a Bible. You can gain a great understanding of the love, grace, and forgiveness of God. You can read stories of others that had a *Face Time* encounter with Him and how that turned out, and you can learn the character and nature of God by learning how He interacted with believers in the past. You can gain an understanding of what God requires of you. You can get to know Him as well as Moses knew Him. This *Face Time* is more than just reading about Him.

You can also talk to Him in prayer. The more you pray, the more you will hear and understand Him, and the more you do that, the more you will experience the love and grace He has for you. No iPhone, Skype, or Internet connection is needed. *Face Time* means spending intimate time in the presence of God, with no outside distractions. This quiet time will lead you to hearing the voice of God speak through the Holy Spirit.

Face Time is a one-on-one encounter with the Father. It's when His Spirit summons you. *Face Time* is so crucial, because it sets the tone for your day. When you start your day before acknowledging Him, it's like going outside to start your car without the key. Christ is the key to unlock every door in your life, every day of your life. The bible shares various examples of *Face Time*.

For example, after Joseph was sold by his brothers into slavery and thrown in a pit, we see how *Face Time* with God enabled Joseph to become the answer to others' problems, even while he was in prison. Daniel had *Face Time* with God after being thrown in the lion's den and God protected Daniel despite being in a near-death situation. Then, we see the miraculous results *Face Time* had in David's life. After he was underestimated as being just *a shepherd boy,* the *Face Time* David had spent with God in previous years, gave him the faith to defeat the giant Goliath.

Each of these people faced a moment of truth—these moments were their turning points, and once they overcame these moments, God elevated them to a level they had never experienced. God used their toughest moments for His glory. No one else could take credit for what God had done. There are situations in your life today (or that will arise in the future) that will require *Face Time.*

You must be ready to take full advantage of your life-changing moments with God. Most *Face Time* encounters change the course of our destiny. Life brings these moments, either by design to propel us to destiny (as was the case with David via Goliath), or to make us confront our own sin, or disobedience.

In addition, attacks from Satan come to destroy us, and during these moments, *Face Time* will be our only saving grace. Many times, moments that require *Face Time* are designed to destroy us when we are not going in the right direction. The good news is that after the encounter, we have an opportunity to start over and get positioned for where God wants us to be. Just like the Israelites in the Bible, *Face Time* moments become our deliverance, where God frees us from the entrapments of this world to set us on the road to our promised land.

The best part is that God predestined us from the beginning so we can't stop his plan, but we can delay ourselves from receiving the harvest of our labor by taking detours or following our own way. We have always heard that there is no testimony without a test. Well it's true, but in order to get to the "testimony," you must get up close and personal with God. I got up close and personal with God during my test, and God's presence gave me peace, despite what I was dealing with in the natural world.

The bible tells us in Daniel 12:4 (KJV) even to the time of the end: many shall run to and fro, and knowledge shall be increased." This has certainly come to pass; however, I believe today's generation has indulged in "information overload" at the sake of a relationship with God. During this information age, often the first thing people do when they wake up in the morning is check emails, text messages, Instagram, Twitter, Snapchat, and Facebook to see how many likes they received overnight.

People subconsciously put their value and worth in the hands of people based on social media likes versus spending *Face Time* with God. People don't want real *Face Time*; they want scheduled time—such as church at 11 a.m. on Sundays. Once that time frame is up, unfortunately, God is kicked to the curb and swapped out for friend requests, selfies and direct messages.

We go through life at such a fast pace—from airplanes, computers, and technology, to the way we converse while texting, with our eyes glued to our phones, rather than to the person we're talking to. Everyone seems to be rushing to check online notifications. We go to work, drop the kids off at school, and we spend hours at salons, barbershops, sporting events, all while recording every moment for others to view.

While many of these tasks seem necessary, they are just distractions that take our attention away from the one source that breathes life into us. As you read through this book, my prayer is that God's words shared to me, as a result of me seeking Him, will inspire you to do the same. We have a direct line to God that never runs out. He is not like your cable connection that interrupts if you don't pay the bill.

Jesus paid our bill over two thousand years ago when he died on the cross so we would never have to worry about being disconnected from the Father. Since "connection" is the nature and way of God, when we experience service interruptions, we immediately know something isn't right. These interruptions come when we allow life to interfere and switch our channels from God.

Distractions such as relationships, media and television, useless or excessive phone conversations, sleeping too much, and even serving in ministry can all cause a disconnect from our *Face Time* with God. It's so important to have balance in our lives. We can sometimes get so involved in serving at church and making sure we are faithful to our local churches, without expanding our relationship with the Creator.

Relationship can only come from intimate moments with God. If we only pick up our bibles and pray at church, how can our relationships with God grow? Most people put so much effort into building human relationships. You may have heard of Author Gary Chapman's book *The Five Love Languages: The Secret to Making Love Last*. It explores the top five languages of love that people respond to.

They include: words of affirmation, acts of service, receiving gifts, quality time, and physical touch. The only way to learn God's "love language" for you is by spending intimate *Face Time* with him. Like Wi-Fi on our cellphones, when you're not in a service area that transmits God, you can't pick up His signal.

When we step outside of His will, we allow ourselves to use unnecessary data because we no longer stay in the service area. This gives the enemy room to hack into our God conscious (or souls) to give us a virus, which often includes depression, lack of peace, joy, faith, and disappointment.

In God's presence, there is fullness. Psalm 16:11(KJV) says, "Thou wilt shew me the path of life: in thy presence is fullness of joy; at thy right hand there are pleasures for evermore." Like a person outside of their cell service area uses "roaming" or costly data on a phone, we sometimes listen to the negative data that enters our minds, when we don't spend *Face Time* with God. We must stay connected to the network of resources God has provided for us so that we won't go offline and get out of His will.

When we abide in His presence, we not only manifest the fruit of His Spirit, but we also gain valuable tools like discernment and faith to help us reject and identify the "viruses" that do not belong. Think about when you are on a computer and you are offline. Your access and connection is limited. This is exactly how it is when you are not connected to God by reading his Word and talking to him in prayer. You are deprived of something that is free to you, and you only get limited access.

It's so important to remember that Jesus is our true and only connection to the Father. If we want to know the will He has for our lives, we must plug in daily through prayer, worship, and meditating on his Word. He is the power source. Just like we charge our iPads and cellphones daily, we must make sure our lives remain at full capacity through *Face Time* with the Lord.

There's No Escaping *Face Time*

I was sound asleep on January 31, 2016, when suddenly my spirit jerked me awake. I popped up, and heard the voice of the Lord speaking to me. He had me turn on a CD called "Withholding Nothing" by William McDowell.

On the song entitled "Releasing the Sound," the singer spoke prophetically before he sang, and his words touched my heart:

"Many have been in a season and place of frustration. You've been sensing that there is more, and you have felt as if you couldn't find me. This is because I am inviting you to find me in a new place. I will not be found in the same old place. Remember I said to the prophet Jeremiah, to my people, 'and you will seek me and find me when you search for me with all your heart and I will be found by you...' For many, you will find that my office is at the end of your rope. When you come to the end of yourself, there you will find me ready to show you things to come. And to place this new mantle for a new sound in you. With this sound will come manifestations and demonstrations of my glory and power. Entire regions will be set free and shifted at once. Nations await. Open your heart to hear, for out of the broken ones will come a sound that will usher in a kingdom revolution within this generation that will reverberate for generations to come and usher in my return."

After that God instructed me to pick up my phone and take notes about what He was saying to me during my worship time… This moment began a long, revealing journey to find myself through God. He was calling me into deeper intimacy with Him. *Face Time* would be required if His words would manifest in my life. I believe we were all created with a divine purpose to impact and change people's lives. I can personally trace my purpose back to a young age. People around me would always say that I was a go-getter and up to something.

This may sound great to some, but not I. See the foremost important thing to me in my younger years was money—and becoming what I considered to be a success. I was so caught up in making money that I lost track of my original purpose. After becoming a teen mom at the age of nineteen, my whole life shifted into survivor mode—I had to do what needed to be done to support myself and my daughter.

This, for me meant sacrificing God's true plan for my life in exchange for corporate and entrepreneurial success. I *had* to land that dream position in my company and become that top money earner in my home-based-businesses. "The grind" enticed me and distracted me for so many years and caused me to depend on myself other than the Creator who had a perfect plan for my life. I faced self-esteem attacks, destiny attacks, social media distractions, spiritual attacks, relationship attacks, and physical attacks that made me the woman I am today.

Feelings of rejection began while growing in school, not feeling good enough and never chosen. These feelings of inadequacy resurfaced after I got pregnant and was rejected by my daughter's father. He said he didn't know if the child was his. He wasn't there to help me raise our child. I began to question why he deserted me, and I thought, *maybe I'm not good enough.* My parents always encouraged me to get an education, so I went to college after high school, but I became pregnant with my daughter during my first year of college.

This didn't stop me. I attended a two-year college and earned my associate degree in accounting. I found my prince charming who accepted this A and B package that I had (me plus my baby girl). I married in my early twenties, purchased my first home by age twenty-four. Years later I went back to school and graduated Magna Cum Laude with my bachelor degree.

I ran a successful internet travel business. In my mind, I was making moves, but something sinister was lurking behind all of that superficial success. In 2010, my perfect world came to a halt, and I divorced my prince charming. I continued my hustle up the corporate ladder, and even had the opportunity to be featured in a TV commercial for Cuyahoga Community College's Job for Joy Enroll campaign.

I also wrote financial articles for the *Phenomenal Woman Magazine*, and I started working as a Financial Advisor for Prudential Advisors, where I achieved "Top Performer" during my first few months. Life was good, or so I thought. The Lord let me know that all of my life experiences had led to that moment—and now it was time for me to first face my own insecurities and then share my experiences to help others.

He told me that it was time to stop searching for answers and realize that I am the answer. God allowed me to endure a teen pregnancy, fairy-tale marriage, a crippling divorce, financial success, low self-esteem, and the biggest challenge of my life— which I will share in the pages that follow. He showed me that through my experiences, He's made me a solution and refuge for others.

I pray this book is an eye-opener to you and causes you to reflect on how much time you spend with the Father. Have you allowed yourself to live in survivor mode? Are you chasing money, a career, and relationships?

The Lord will return soon to establish His kingdom on earth, and I've decided that if I don't achieve another worldly business endeavor, if I don't ever remarry, or if people don't accept me, the most important part of life is to know that when He returns He will find me doing what He has ordained and called me to be, which is a worshipper and an influencer within the Kingdom of God.

Nothing else in life matters. Everything else will soon pass away, but only what we do for Christ will last. I pray *Face Time* provokes you to act today to increase your intimate time with the Father. Follow me as we begin a journey toward destiny.

Questions to Consider When Spending Face Time

What currently distracts you from spending more Face Time with God?

_____

_____

_____

_____

_____

_____

_____

_____

_____

_____

_____

_____

_____

_____

_____

_____

_____

_____

_____

_____

How often do you tap into God's wireless frequencies since he is everywhere? Is it just during a church service? Just during Praise Team/choir rehearsal?

_____

_____

_____

_____

_____

_____

_____

_____

_____

_____

_____

_____

_____

_____

_____

_____

_____

_____

_____

_____

When was your last Face Time Encounter with God? Did he knock and you not answer?

_____

_____

_____

_____

_____

_____

_____

_____

_____

_____

_____

_____

_____

_____

_____

_____

_____

_____

Chapter 2

Code Blue

"Your life was spinning in so many directions, like a vicious twister tornado, not knowing everything in your path would be destroyed if you didn't soon take cover."

I couldn't walk. I couldn't talk. Breathing through my nose and mouth seemed like the hardest feat ever. These symptoms let me know that I couldn't wait any longer. I rushed to the hospital to face my fate. My blood pressure rapidly increased and the doctors and nurses rushed to strap me onto a bed and plug in the oxygen machines. The beeping, the scurry, the voices around me were controlled, yet urgent.

It was just like a dramatic hospital sitcom, or movie, only this was real, and it was me who was the cause of concern. *Is this the beginning of the end?* I thought. As the possibility of death began to invade my thoughts and as my imagination took a wrong turn toward defeat, God stepped in, and declared, *"Not so. This is my daughter who I ordained to LIVE and proclaim the gospel for my glory.*

This episode started one bitter, cold Monday morning in January. I woke up and was called to begin my *"Face Time"* journey into a destination that I would have never imagined would shift my entire life forever. In November, 2015 after returning from a fabulous ten-day vacation in the Caribbean islands, I became ill in my body—my feet swollen. Walking and standing were extremely uncomfortable. I brushed it off and thought it was a flare of fibromyalgia. I had been dealing with pain from that irritating condition for the previous four years, on and off.

I hated going to the doctor, so I decided to just keep life moving and elevate my feet in hopes that the swelling would eventually subside. Weeks passed, and it was Christmas Eve when my feet began to look like Ms. Piggy from the *Muppets.* You would think this would be cause for alarm, but not for me. I kept going, business as usual, and didn't slow down. Instead, with swollen feet, I headed to my daughter's house to wrap Christmas gifts for my granddaughters.

My daughter's friend, who is a registered nurse, observed my feet and legs, which looked like Elephant Man. "That looks like hypodermia or something with your kidneys," she said. I immediately rushed to the hospital on Christmas Eve to learn that I had inflammation in both feet. That following Tuesday on December 30th, I followed up with my rheumatologist, who looked at my feet and immediately informed me that it was not just fibromyalgia.

He was confident in his diagnosis, "Lupus is attacking your kidneys." He immediately contacted my nephrologist, and I called the scheduler at the University Hospitals of Cleveland, Ohio to schedule an appointment for a kidney biopsy. *This is just routine,* I thought. At first, she scheduled my surgery for January 8th.

Apparently, no beds were available. January 11th was the new available date for my surgery. After that, I received another call saying I could not have the procedure until I had a consultation with the physician. I would not take "no" for an answer. I begged and pleaded with the hospital worker, because by this time, the worry from my family and nephrologist made me feel like I should get this matter resolved quickly.

I believe that the hospital scheduler was a guardian angel, because he went above and beyond his pay grade to get a clearance so that I could have the consultation waived and get the procedure done by another doctor. His gesture ended up saving my life, because had I not been admitted into the hospital for a biopsy on January 11th, I would have died, according to my doctor.

My kidneys started failing and it began to look as if I was dying slowly. They went from functioning at ninety-five percent in September to twenty-four percent the day I was admitted. The doctors thought I was having a heart attack. The first attempt to do the biopsy procedure didn't even take, because they could not get a clear picture of my kidneys. The biopsy didn't reveal enough.

They attempted to do the procedure again on Thursday, January 14th, but my blood pressure had escalated to over 270 at this point, so it was another failed attempt. I was experiencing shortness of breath and I was on oxygen machines. I couldn't walk, barely talk, but despite it all, I felt God's presence and heard his voice. The enemy was trying to take his final shot. He wanted my life, and he hit me with a surprise blow.

On some days, I would wake up with eight or nine doctors standing over my bed looking at me as if I was a science project gone bad. Their faces told the story—doom and gloom. It wouldn't be too much longer until they could pull the plug, *or so they thought.* Physically, I was weak, but my spirit man had not given up hope.

I knew I had to go deeper in the Spirit and stay connected to God. During my hospital stay, the Lord sent true prayer warriors to my bedside, such as local pastors and apostles, my family in faith and good girlfriends who are also my prayer partners. Each night when my family, church family, and close friends left, I pulled out my iPad and listened to praise and worship songs, because I knew that praise was my weapon.

I listened to Cindy Trimm's Healing prayer on YouTube and fell asleep while speaking healing over my body. I was determined to be healed from the lupus that had attacked my kidneys. I covered myself in a prayer cloth that my cousin gave me. I took communion every night before laying down, and I was confident that God's word was true: *"You can't have this one. She has destiny and kingdom assignments to complete."*

As my one hundred-year-old grandfather Lewis Riley would say, "Ain't Nobody God, but God." The Lord raised me up out of that hospital bed. After, six months in the hospital—a biopsy, breathing treatments, two blood transfusions and several scares with diabetes—I was finally released from the hospital once in for all… or so I thought. The next scare took me by surprise.

It was a beautiful, Sunday July afternoon in Ohio. I had just come home from church, and I was playing outside with my granddaughters. Suddenly, my hands and arms went numb, then my feet. My hands started to shake, and my face felt really strange. Then, I couldn't speak. I was immediately re-admitted into the hospital. My speech was gone for a few hours.

On that afternoon, I had a stroke. The hospital once again became my home for three gruesome days. I left the hospital to stay in the loving care of my parents' home until I was more stabilized, but my fight wasn't over. My days and nights were difficult. Depression came knocking at my doorstep, and I wondered when I could experience a normal day of no pain.

I cried out to God in my weakest moments, in between fifteen different medications, I shouted out to him, and He responded: *"I'm not done with you. I need you to know why this all happened."* I was starting to understand that the Lord did not bring this sickness upon me, but he allowed the enemy to attack my body, so that He might be glorified. Just like Job in the bible, the enemy petitioned God regarding Job, and the Lord said he could bring calamities in his life, but he could not take his life.

Satan thought Job would curse God, but instead it just increased his intimate relationship with the Father. It allowed him to know that God was still with him no matter what attacks the enemy put in Job's path. I had heard of the story of Job preached for years, but after my own experience, it became real. I could see that this was just a testing of my faith.

More Face Time between the Father and I was required. The only weapon I had against the attacks in my body were praise and worship—intimate time with my Creator and Healer. I then set out on a mission to learn the reason for my attack. I discovered that my experience was a wakeup call that my life was moving in the wrong direction.

My issue was that I was moving too fast, trying to be too much for everyone, and focused on business, making money, and everyone else, not my own well-being. During my recovery, I worshipped in my room during the day, and each night I spent *Face Time* with God. He began to give me different assignments for my life.

He gave me clear instructions for my financial services business, for completing a song on healing that He placed in my heart on New Year's Eve. God works in mysterious ways. He had already spoken to me about my healing through this song, prior to me being admitted to the hospital, before I ever knew what was wrong with me. This was a song God gave me after I had went to the hospital on Christmas Eve with feet swollen.

During my hospital visit on Christmas Eve, the physicians misdiagnosed me and said I had inflammation. They instructed me to follow up with my primary physician. Weeks passed before I could get an appointment. I sat in church very uncomfortable that night, and I could not stand during praise and worship. I was very weak.

After church I walked to my car, turned on a CD my sister had given me, and as I listened to the long instrumental intro, I sang, "Lord you are my healer…" I was very full at this point, almost in tears singing. God gave me the words to my song as I waited to leave the church parking lot.

Since I attend a mega church, it takes forever to get out of the parking lot. That's how God birthed my prophetic song on healing. I was truly overwhelmed by God's glory. One day, just weeks earlier, I was on my death bed, and now, here I was receiving revelations from God.

He told me that I had the gift of healing, and that he would do exceedingly abundantly above all I could ever ask or think in my life. One morning, God woke me up and said, *"I declare this day my child you are healed from every infirmity that attacked your body; you are healed from every medication that entered your body and altered it."* I immediately ran in the kitchen and told my parents that I was healed. "I'm healed in Jesus' name.

God said that I'm healed, not only from this sickness, but every sickness that ever tried to attack me mentally, emotionally, and through bad relationships!" He said, *"For every tear you cried, I'm about to restore double for your trouble like I did for Elijah."* I told my parents God told me I was healed in Jesus name.

"There was a reason for all the pain you have endured in your life. It was all to get you to this point in your life, so I could have FaceTime with you. Rise up my daughter go forth. You are finally free. Whom the son sets free is free indeed, and I call you free to speak to the north, south, east, west, and declare that I am the God of Isaac, Jacob, and Abraham. I am sending you out in my name, not for fame and fortune, but so that others may know beyond a shadow of a doubt that surely nobody but God could have done this. You will speak to many nations and they will know I have sent you. My child, I told you that the last shall be first, and the first shall be last. Now is your time to come from the background and stand front and center to let the world know I am the God your healer.

"I am Jehovah Rapha, I am Jehovah Shalom, I am Jehovah your Protector, and I will be with you in every step you take. No weapon formed against you shall prosper. (Isaiah 54:17) Tell the world you are healed on this night. I have spoken. It is done, in Jesus' name. I am the healer of the world. I formed this world without any shape. It was void with no life, but I spoke it into existence and it was. I am that I am and always will be. Thank you for our Face Time."

The Lord allowed me to travel into a place I had never been in the spiritual realm. In this place, I had dominion and authority to speak of things and they came to pass. During a breakfast conversation one morning during this same time, my dad reminded me of a comment my pastor Dr. R.A. Vernon of The Word Church preached, "Alisa, ask God for what you want," my dad said. So I began to speak boldly to every situation.

God had placed a realm of favor over me. I began to ask God for things, and they just happened. It was a season of open Heaven, a time when you can ask God for anything. When we get into such an intimate place with the Father we begin to understand who we are and the authority we walk in. Our deeper knowledge of our true authority helps us to no longer settle for less.

We realize that our inheritance gives us so much access. When you accept the Lord in your life, you become a joint heir to the throne. The bible says that the earth is the Lord's and the fullness thereof. (Psalms 24:1) Since the Lord owns it all, we have access. I began to see why I had went through so much pain and rejection in my life.

I realize God doesn't send sickness, but He is able to turn it all around for my good. I also realized that in the end, the things that I have experienced are not about me. The victory helps everyone else after me. Now, I have empathy for others, because I have experienced these types of attacks myself. What I considered my misery has become my ministry.

I see now if I had never been a teen mom, I couldn't relate to teens getting pregnant and not being married. If I had not experienced the rejection as a child, while on praise teams and in other groups, I wouldn't understand true rejection. My experiences now allow me to glorify God through my testimony.

My pain helped me become the answer to so many people's problems. If I had not endured my trials, I would not be qualified to now be the answer. If I had not experienced sickness, perhaps I would have never realized that I too have the gift of healing.

I now lay hands on people and pray boldly in the Spirit, and others experience healing as well. *"I need you to spend more FaceTime with me,"* says the Lord. One morning during my healing process, the Lord entered my inner being and spoke to me. He said, *"My daughter, I gave you life back. Now go live. Your life was spinning in so many directions, like a vicious twister tornado, not knowing everything in your path would be destroyed if you didn't soon take cover.*

My child you were going too fast in so many directions trying to build a business, care for your elderly parents, be the best girlfriend you could be, be a good mom, and be a good grandmother. There you go again trying to be everything to everybody, but never loving yourself. You forgot to realize that if you don't stop and take time to breathe, you will crash. So since you would not stop, I had to stop you, my child, because I have too much for you to do for the kingdom. Your intentions were great, but you were going in the wrong direction. That was not the course I had set for your life. Think it not strange that your battles in life were so intense?

That's because I graced you for it all. I have ordained you from the beginning of time, before you were formed in your mother's womb. Think it not strange that you have always been unique. You have always been a seer, a visionary—as a child, you always saw past what others could see; you always believed you had hope against hope. You were never average. My daughter, don't apologize for who you are and how you think. You were originally designed and handcrafted in my image. You will never be average.

You have had to fight all your life. My child I have always loved you, but you didn't realize the extent of my love for you. You allowed others to define you and tell you who you should be. I made you exactly who I wanted you to be. Don't you realize and see now why you have always been under attack? The enemy saw the greatness in you and that's why he tried to kill you several times.

Remember when you went on the family vacation to PTL and almost drowned in the swimming pool? You tried to show your sisters and brothers that you could float backwards with a kick, and you kicked out into the water, six-feet-deep. You were always a prankster as a child, so they thought you were crying wolf...

But even then as you were drowning, I saved you, and I told you to start swimming like a fish. And when you were on vacation in St. Thomas Virgin Islands [in 2002], and you decided to be that same adventurous person, still unable to swim. You mounted a jet ski, and while riding, the driver made a sharp turn. The jet ski flipped over on you, and you almost drowned, but I saved you again.

I sent a nice couple who sent for help to rescue you. What about the time you were almost hit by a truck coming around I-77? Your car was nearly crushed, but I sent my angels to literally pick your car up and move it out of the semi truck's way. Remember the times you drove out of town for trips and business conferences and fell asleep at the wheel of the car?

My hand of mercy has always been on you my child. The call on your life is so great that I couldn't let anything or anyone take you out of here, before you completed my assignments on your life. And now this last near-death experience was all to draw you back to me."

Questions to consider for Physical Attacks:

Do you ever think your Superwoman or Superman, and you can eat any kind of way, not get enough sleep or exercise?

What type of balance do you have in your life? (Is your life the same ritual work, home, school, church etc.)

_____

_____

_____

_____

_____

_____

_____

_____

_____

_____

_____

_____

_____

_____

_____

_____

_____

_____

How can you avoid stressful situations? Are you currently involved in an abusive (emotionally/mentally) relationship?

_____

_____

_____

_____

_____

_____

_____

_____

_____

_____

_____

_____

_____

_____

_____

_____

_____

_____

_____

Who or what have you allowed to define who you are?

_____

_____

_____

_____

_____

_____

_____

_____

_____

_____

_____

_____

_____

_____

_____

_____

_____

_____

_____

_____

_____

Chapter 3

Self Esteem Attacks

"The enemy knows our great potential, and his job is to assassinate our destinies, before we even get wind of them."

We live in a world where people are so pressured to be perfect, look perfect, Photoshop this; crop this, getting surgeries to change this. If we are not careful comparing ourselves to others can cause self-esteem attacks. The dictionary defines self-esteem as confidence in one's own worth or abilities; self-respect. Don't get me wrong keep that hair slayed, body in shape, etc but we must not allow the world's definition of beauty to define us. My Mom always told me, "Beauty is only skin deep".

Everyone will age at some point, and no face lifts or makeovers will matter. We can very easily begin focusing on ourselves and not on God. This is one of the ways Satan distracts us from God's will for our lives. People focus on their faults and weakness so much, and wonder why they aren't happy, but it's because they have an inner war going on with themselves. We must realize we are not a finished product.

I had to learn to accept myself faults and all. Don't go around being against yourself. We must look at ourselves through the lens of Christ. We can only gain confidence in our true selves by spending *Face Time* with our heavenly Father.

That is where we can understand how God sees us. Psalms 139:13-16 (MSG) tells us "Oh yes, you shaped me first inside, then out; you formed me in my mother's womb. I thank you High God-you're breathtaking! Body and soul, I am marvelously made! I worship in adoration-what a creation! As we spend Face Time we become confident and bold.

Many people who suffer from self-esteem attacks can experience extreme fear and anxiety frequently. At times they can believe that there is something wrong with themselves. When they do something they feel to have been stupid, something they think others have noticed, and something that confirms their own feelings of inadequacy, incompetence, being undeserving or unlovable.

During these attacks they may withdraw and isolate while feeling embarrassed, humiliated, devastated, depressed, and even despairing. Many people who are struggling with self-confidence sometimes become either overachievers or underachievers. Some people are frustrated and feel pressured to prove their adequacy-often becoming very successful as the result of their lack of self-esteem.

Some people that are fighting these attacks can remain in unsatisfying or abusive relationships, stay on jobs where there is no opportunity for advancement and a lack of employee benefits, put their dreams on hold, and go through life convinced that trying to make a change will result in disappointment, humiliation, or being alone.

People who lack self-confidence tend to be needy. These are limiting beliefs low self-esteem sufferers repeat over and over. This can also lead to many forms of obsessive-compulsive or addictive behaviors. Often trying to feel better about themselves, those experiencing self-esteem attacks may become involved in addictive spending, perfectionism, drug abuse, excessive drinking, and various sexual relationships trying to fill a void.

As a child growing up, I experienced a lot of rejection. I can recall being in elementary school always being the last one picked for teams. I was always criticized for my size. The other students would call me Olive Oil, pop bottle, flat-chested, and say that I was too skinny. The guys would often tell me I had a cute face, and if I had a better body I would be the whole package.

I was cracked on about my forehead and thin frame. I allowed these words and painful memories to linger in my head for years. At the time not realizing that having my spirit broken was part of my process. During the summer of the sixth grade, I was riding my bike with my sister and fell off the handle bars to avoid being hit by an oncoming car.

I hit my head on the concrete, so I walked home and immediately sat at the kitchen table and laid my head down to elevate the pain. This ended up being a really bad idea. I fell into a comma and was unconscious for three days. My parents later told me that the doctors said I wouldn't make it, but God once again stepped in and said *not so, not now she has work to do.*

This was another *Face Time* encounter with God, where He raised me up miraculously out of a comatose state. All of my childhood experiences that were meant for evil to deter my destiny all worked out for my good. (Romans 8:28).

I could now see how it was all used to build my character, so I could become the woman I am today. My life is a true testament to the saying, "My mess became my ministry. "As I grew older, I began to volunteer for more leadership roles at school, including the captain of various sports and extracurricular teams. Despite the rejection I experienced early-on, my confidence was increasing.

I started to answer questions first during class, and I became more involved in school youth groups. I remember my first solo with the youth choir. We were invited to sing at the House of Corrections, a local correctional facility for a Christmas program, and I sang a song and received an encore. That day changed my life and increased my confidence for singing. From that point on, I started singing publicly.

I even had the opportunity to sing with a group on the Bobby Jones Gospel show. As I grew older, I ministered with several praise teams, but each time, I was suppressed or made to feel like my gift was not good enough or my anointing was not like others. This continued with every team I joined, but I still worshipped on my own and let God birth prophetic songs during church services or during my long solo drives in the car.

I learned a lesson from these experiences. When God has something for us, and it's not quite our time, He must keep us hidden in the background. The enemy knows our great potential, and his job is to assassinate our destinies, before we even get wind of them. As I grew into adulthood, I spent many years feeling inadequate and never quite good enough.

I always felt like I had to prove I had a right to my space. Many times we over give, over commit, over excuse, over compensate, and stay in difficult desperate situations much longer than it is wise or productive to do so.

I spent years trying to be everything to everybody. However, I never tended to my own needs. I felt that I always had to do more than everybody else to be noticed. I used to see others and think *why can't I just meet the status quo, like them, and just do enough to get by?* The Lord let me know that He didn't create me to be average.

He let me know He allowed my spirit to be broken so that I would strive to be *above average*. If He allowed me to be content, I would have missed my destiny. I soon realized that I had to learn to love and accept myself where I was. In spite of all my imperfections, I was created as God's original design.

All I needed was validation from God, and not man. Rejection is not a sign of inferiority, but it is a sign that you need to move on. It means that, that person or relationship no longer has the capacity to support your purpose and your destiny. I had to learn to not cry when I am rejected, but I had to learn to give myself a going away party. A crisis is a divine announcement that God wants you to move to the next realm.

Once I got this revelation I begin to rejoice over the people that left my lives. Like the saying goes, "Let the doorknob hit ya where the dog should have bit ya". I began to look at myself in the mirror every day and speak daily positive affirmations, and tell myself what God says about me.

I told myself I deserve to be happy and successful, I am worthy, I am beautifully and wonderfully made, I deserve to be loved, I am flexible and open to change in my life. Know who you are in Christ. You must build up your confidence and self-esteem. This can only happen by reading His Word daily.

After we have spent *Face Time* with God we must also utilize and attend classes such as grief recovery, mother/father wounds, counseling with a psychologist, or support groups.

Sometimes past wounds are so deep, and we can't be too "spiritual" (to our own detriment) and think everything will happen through prayer. Yes, healing comes through fasting and prayer, but God also created doctors, because sometimes our minds have been imprisoned for so long it will take prayer and counseling to help us heal.

Reading motivational books, driving and listening to motivational CD's, and surrounding yourself with like-minded people are other ways to build up your self-esteem. How can eagles hang around pigeons? I always say misery loves company.

You don't have time to hang around negative people or dream stealers, because they are like magnets. Soon you will become negative—full of doubt and begin to second guess yourself as well. Be encouraged you've come along way.

You may have a lot of areas you still struggle with, but being against yourself is not going to help you. Let God continue to make and mold you into who he created you to be.

Don't listen to the condemning voices inside. God loves you with an everlasting love that has nothing to do with your qualifications. I encourage you to shake off the guilt of unworthiness and put on the breastplate of God's approval. If God approves you then you don't need validation by anyone else.

Question for Self Esteem Attacks

Has your self-esteem been attacked? If so, think back on your journey and consider the lessons that God wants you to learn from your experiences.

_____

_____

_____

_____

_____

_____

_____

_____

_____

_____

_____

_____

_____

_____

_____

_____

_____

_____

_____

_____

What lies are you listening to about yourself? Have you considered the source?

_____

_____

_____

_____

_____

_____

_____

_____

_____

_____

_____

_____

_____

_____

_____

_____

_____

_____

_____

_____

_____

_____

_____

_____

As children we came into this world believing we could do anything, who did you allow to come into your life to change your impression of yourself?

_____

_____

_____

_____

_____

_____

_____

_____

_____

_____

_____

_____

_____

_____

_____

_____

_____

_____

_____

_____

When you look in your mirror, who do you see? Is it who God said you are or who someone else defined you to be?

_____

_____

_____

_____

_____

_____

_____

_____

_____

_____

_____

_____

_____

_____

_____

_____

_____

_____

_____

_____

_____

How often do you celebrate yourself? (Take yourself to a movie or out to dinner etc.)

_____

_____

_____

_____

_____

_____

_____

_____

_____

_____

_____

_____

_____

_____

_____

_____

_____

_____

_____

Chapter 4

Destiny Attacks

"Failing to understand my purpose caused me to take many unnecessary detours"

Has your entire world ever felt under attack? There were so many times when my destiny was under attack, and I could feel it. Whenever you have been called to do something great for the kingdom expect certain things to be planted in your life as a tool to abort what God was going to do in your life.

When God has invested greatness inside of you expect the enemy to cause a conflict in your garden. Look at Adam and Eve in the Garden of Eden they had been given access to so much and then came the enemy to distract and tempt them to try to abort their destiny.

The enemy only attacks people approaching their season. It's like a pregnant woman, the closer she gets to giving birth the more intense the contractions become. The doctors watch to see how many centimeters she has dilated, which lets them know she is almost right at the verge of birthing something.

It's the same for us. Think it not strange when things get more intense in your life, these are final tests to see if you will cross over or have to wait some more years in the wilderness like the children of Israel wandering in the desert for 40 years.

Destiny attacks can be brought on by personal bad decisions, disobedience, or Satan himself. I have always desired to serve the Lord with all my heart, but, blinded, I often allowed fatal distractions to delay my path. "And we know that in all things God works for the good of those who love him, who have been called according to his purpose" Romans 8:28 (NIV).

The Lord also gives us free will, and if we choose a path of sin and destruction, that is what we will receive. For quite some time, it seemed each time I made up in my mind that I was going to serve the Lord, I would start off strong, at the top of the year—reading my One Year Bible, listening to praise and worship music, beginning my day in prayer, and everything would be going fine. Then I would allow things or people to distract me from my *Face Time* with Him.

Sometimes, I became obsessed with my career or a new business opportunity and put God on the backburner. I was truly distracted, and my "all-in" personality trait caused me to put my all into those business projects, not realizing that I had forsaken my *Face Time* with the Lord. I'm either all the way in or all the way out.

There is no in between with me. I would go to work, focus on meeting goals, work so hard during the day, and then by the time I came home to what we call "wine down time," that was all she wrote. I would wake up the next day and the rat race just continued. It was a vicious cycle of get up, read a quick scripture, go to work, allow things to stress me out, and forget the power of God's Word.

Other catastrophic distractions were my relationships with men. After a seventeen-year marriage, followed by a devastating divorce, I began to long for companionship. Once I started dating someone, I was all in. Everything became about making my relationship great.

It got to a point that I spent so much time focused on my earthly relationship that I began to spend less time working on my intimate relationship with the Father. I would spend so much time texting or talking on the phone to a man, dedicating more time to him than my heavenly Father.

I wanted to walk in my destiny, but I didn't always apply the promise in Matthew 6:33(NIV) to my life, which states, "But seek first his kingdom and his righteousness, and all these things will be given to you as well." Too often, I settled for men who were not even on the same spiritual level as I was, because I wanted their companionship. I am not alone in this.

It's human nature to sometimes stay with partners who are bad for us, because we don't want to be alone. When we do this, we devalue ourselves. I would make excuses like, "Well at least he knows the Lord and goes to church."

"At least he watches *Preachers* with me on television or The Word Network." The bible says in Matthew 7:16 (NIV) that by their fruit you will recognize them, and as time progressed, I saw these relationships for what they were—fleshly. They were not heavenly rooted with a strong (or true) foundation in the Lord. Immediately after watching "the Word" on television, these guys would still want to have sex with me.

I had the nerve to make excuses for these men, and myself. I convinced myself that perhaps they weren't as strong in the Lord as me, but they still feared God. The reality is if they truly feared God and had the indwelling of the Holy Spirit, they would have felt the same guilt that I felt after intimacy. Yes, we all want to be and feel love from another human being, but sexual intimacy was truly made for a husband and wife who have made a commitment and covenant before God. I wanted God and a "Boo." The bible says, "No other gods, only me."

Exodus 20:3 (MSG) whether it's a job, family, a Boo, we can't allow anything to come before our relationship and *Face Time* with God. Anything that interferes with that is a distraction and affects our destiny. If you've wondered why you may not have achieved all the dreams God showed you in a vision, it may be because somewhere you allowed other stuff to get in the way. Failing to understand my purpose caused me to take many unnecessary detours.

The Lord had a clear direction for my life, but I tried to lead and not follow his plan. I went through a season of identity theft, where I forgot who I was in Christ. I'm a person that was raised in the church all my life. I memorized scriptures from a young child, but I allowed the cares of life to shift me into a person I barely recognized. Things I would have never tolerated I found myself accepting. It's so important to know why you were created before you start trying to determine your destiny. God created us to know him and to have an intimate personal relationship with him.

Even though this relationship was lost when Adam and Eve sinned in the Garden of Eden, when you accept Jesus into your life it restores the relationship. Spending *Face Time* with God is vital to understanding your destiny. When you don't have this intimate relationship with God, you will seek to fulfill your destiny from wrong motives, such as fear, insecurity, money, relationships, etc.

As you spend Face Time he will begin to reveal your destiny. Jeremiah 29:11(NIV) tells us "For I know the plans I have for you, declares the Lord, plans to prosper you and not to harm you, plans to give you hope and a future." Our purpose is chosen by God. It's not open to discussion. We may cause our journey to be extended due to decisions we make. I can recall having to repeat a test so many times, because I kept failing the process so many times due to my own disobedience.

I could have saved myself so much time if I had been spending intimate time with God. That is why it's so important to avoid things and people that contradict his purpose for your life. Our destiny is attached to doing the will of God. So anything that distracts you from that is a definite attack against your destiny. The purpose of *Face Time* with God is to bring awareness to the various things that can creep into our lives that can delay us from walking into our destiny.

If we truly realized how much God loves us, we will realize that He knows what is best for us and he also knows the perfect timing to deliver our blessings. My *Face Time* journey led me back to my first love, which is spending intimate time with the Father. There is nothing like it or anything in the world that can replace it. There is no hobby, stress reliever, self-medication or pleasure that can replace true alone time with God... Believe me, I've tried them!

Questions for Destiny Attacks

Have you allowed the enemy to use condemnation to stop you from moving forward? If so repent to God and move forward.

_____

_____

_____

_____

_____

_____

_____

_____

_____

_____

_____

_____

_____

_____

_____

_____

_____

_____

_____

_____

Are you looking back on your past or focusing on your future and things you have control of?

_____

_____

_____

_____

_____

_____

_____

_____

_____

_____

_____

_____

_____

_____

_____

_____

_____

_____

_____

_____

How persistent are you? Do you allow "No" to keep you from your destiny?

_____

_____

_____

_____

_____

_____

_____

_____

_____

_____

_____

_____

_____

_____

_____

_____

_____

_____

Do you attend a biblically-sound church? Where the Word is taught and God's Spirit dwell? If you are attending a church focused on entertainment, fluff, or rituals, leave in search of one where the Word is rightly divided.

How are you receiving your daily spiritual food?

_____

_____

_____

_____

_____

_____

_____

_____

_____

_____

_____

_____

_____

_____

_____

_____

_____

_____

Chapter 5

Spiritual Attacks

"God is our GPS powered step-by-step guide that tells us exactly what to do if we give him Face Time."

God wants our undivided attention. He wants exclusive rights. Just like when you're in a committed relationship you give that person exclusivity, the same is required for a relationship with God. When He has our attention, He gives us the orders for our lives. When we spend intimate time with God, He can reveal so much to us. *Face Time* is quality time with God, and this quality time will help us fight and win the spiritual attacks.

We learn God's ways by spending intimate time with Him. If we just open our Word while we are at church on Sunday and never open it again until the next Sunday, we will miss so much of what He wants to share with us. We go to a gas station each week to fuel our cars, because we know if we run out of gas, the car will not start. We must spend *Face Time* with Him so that we stay full of his Spirit.

The bible says "Now the Lord is that spirit; and where the Spirit of the Lord is, there is liberty," 2 Corinthians 3:17 (KJV). If we truly want to be free in our minds and experience a liberated life we need to connect with Him daily, even hourly. He is our source and strength.

When Jesus died on the cross and after he ascended back to heaven, He said He was leaving His comforter with us, and that is His Holy Spirit. (John 14:15-17) We have the advantage of having all three parts of God. We had the Father in the beginning when the earth was void and He spoke everything into existence. Then we had His Son, Jesus, whom He sent into the world to be a ransom for our sins, and now we have the Holy Spirit—our comforter and guide, until God returns again to establish his kingdom on earth.

The beautiful thing about having all three parts of the Godhead is that we have each, simultaneously all the time. God is with us in more ways than you and I can imagine. If we don't connect with Him daily, we lose a part of the true intimacy that God had intended for us. In the bible, in 1 Chronicles 4:10 (NIV) says, "Lord I need your help, Oh that you would bless me and enlarge my territory! Let your hand be with me, and keep me from harm so that I will be free from pain." And God granted his request.

We ask the Lord for so much; a spouse, better job, more finances, it's like 'Lord gimme gimme, gimme,' but when do we just come to God and thank him for who He is—the King of Kings, Lord of Lords, El Shaddai, Jehovah Shalom, Jehovah Jireh, and Jehovah Rapha? God's will is that you may enjoy good health and that all may go well with you, even as your soul is getting along well (3 John 1:2 NIV). Most people read that scripture and stay on the first part about prospering, but you can only prosper as your soul prospers.

Our soul can only prosper as you spend one-on-one time with him. Each year, I see so many people saying what they are going to do differently after the New Year, and so many resolutions remain unfulfilled. The reason is because they start the year off with God. They are just like I was.

We start with first fruit offerings to God: we fast, pray, tithe, worship, meditate... but as the year progresses, we allow the cares of life to take precedence in our lives. We pray less, worship less, and spend five quick minutes reading our One Year Bibles/devotionals. Soon the first fruit become leftovers. God is treated like second-hand clothing. Meanwhile, we can spend hours a day talking with a girlfriend, boyfriend, or gossip buddy. We must stop. We must stop spending hours watching reality television, our favorite sports teams, Lifetime movies, or HGTV series' in replace of spending quality time with God.

There is nothing wrong with entertainment, but God just wants exclusivity. He wants to be first. God realizes you have a family. You may be a single mom or single dad, a busy college student, a newlywed, or a business owner. God gave you these blessings, and He understands they require your attention, but in order for your horizontal relationships to grow, your vertical relationship with God must be tight. The bible says, "But seek first his kingdom and his righteousness, and all these things will be given to you as well," (Matthew 6:33 NIV).

If we seek His face and put Him first, everything else will follow. Think about Solomon, a great man of wisdom in the Bible. He had so much material wealth—probably more than we could possibly imagine, but when God asked him what he wanted, he didn't ask for more stuff. He just wanted wisdom, because he knew that wisdom was the key to unlock all of his hearts desires (see 1 Kings 3:4-10). Wisdom is the spiritual currency Solomon used. He didn't need to chase money, fortune, or fame—all of that came, because he tapped into wisdom.

God has prepared such an awesome life for you and me. He's just waiting for us to spend *Face Time* so he can reveal himself and the plans He has for our lives. When we go through life without intimacy with the Father, we become like a ship without a sail.

God wants to be the captain of our lives. He wants to maneuver the controls of our lives, so that we aren't just tossed and guided by the unstable seas of life. Sometimes in life we go through identity theft. Which means you forget who and whose you are in Christ. When this happens it causes us to become something or pursue something that is totally outside our character. We began to make quick and haste decisions based on the person we have become for that moment. I'm a living witness of someone stealing your identity.

My identity was stolen and someone got credit in my name in another state. This caused me to have to file papers to prove I was who I said I was. It's bad when you know who you are, but have to show your ID to prove it. God told you how great you were and what he called you to be, but because you took on a new identity you now have to do things you never would have had to do just to prove yourself. I had to file alerts to protect my credit.

The Lord tries to alert us when he sees we have allowed the enemy to steal our identity. Are you listening to the alerts or are you so caught up in the new false identity that you forgot who God truly called you to be. I encourage you to seek God daily, so there is no mistake as to who you are. The bible tells us in Proverbs 3:6 (KJV) to acknowledge the Lord in all our ways and he shall direct your path.

It's a real spiritual battle in this world. The enemy is seeking who he may devour. If you have fallen away spiritually and forgot who you are it's not too late to come back to your true identity in Christ. The Lord loved you so much to send you signs and alerts that you're not moving in the right direction. I encourage you right now wherever you are to bow down and open your mouth and ask the Lord to make you over.

To "create in me a pure heart, Oh God, and renew a steadfast spirit within me" Psalms 51:10 (NIV). It's never too late no matter what you've done or who you've done it with. The Lord is just waiting to spend Face Time with you. His mercy and grace is so sufficient. He can help to guard you against all the spiritual darts that come your way that want to steal your life. You have more power and authority than you know.

Put the phone down and turn off the TV and spend some time with me says the Lord. I am your source...I am your peace...I am your hope. This is why daily time with the Father is a necessity, not an option. When you leave home, you don't forget your cellphone. We must take the Lord with us everywhere we go. The Lord is our GPS. God is our powered step-by-step guide that tells us exactly what to do if we give him *Face Time*.

When we meet with Him and enter our destination, He begins to speak and navigate our course. He helps us to avoid roadblocks, which include bad decisions, bad relationships choices, or bad people. God prevents us from making mistakes — and when we do mess up; He patiently helps us find our way back. That means we're never pushed to do the difficult work of recalculating for ourselves.

If you're reading this book, and saying 'I want to experience a *Face Time* encounter with God of my own,' just stop what you're doing right now, raise your hands and seek him. Jeremiah 29:13 (NIV) promises, "You will seek me and find me when you seek me with all your heart."

Questions for Spiritual Attacks

How often do you get in a quiet place, turn off your cellphone television, and take a break from social media?

_____

_____

_____

_____

_____

_____

_____

_____

_____

_____

_____

_____

_____

_____

_____

_____

_____

_____

Does your Boo or spouse have more exclusivity than God?

What weapons are you using to fight against spiritual attacks? (Listening to worship music, praying in the spirit, verbally speaking God's word out loud, all of this works as a shield against spiritual attacks)

_____

_____

_____

_____

_____

_____

_____

_____

_____

_____

_____

_____

_____

_____

_____

_____

_____

_____

Are you reading your bible daily? Whether it's the One Year Bible, You Version Bible app, both are great resources.

_____

_____

_____

_____

_____

_____

_____

_____

_____

_____

_____

_____

_____

_____

_____

_____

_____

_____

_____

_____

_____

What are your daily thoughts? It's so important what you put into your ear and eye gates. The Bible tells us we wrestle not against flesh and blood, but against the rulers, against the authorities Ephesians 6:12 NIV

_____

_____

_____

_____

_____

_____

_____

_____

_____

_____

_____

_____

_____

_____

_____

_____

_____

Closing Thoughts

I begin my days opening the Bible App and reading my daily scripture, saying a prayer, and by listening to my favorite worship singers, because I have found that praise and worship sets the tone for my intimate experience with the Lord. As you begin to sing and let the words saturate your lips, the Holy Spirit will now have access to your heart and mind.

I have learned that I must shut out all outside influences, because *Face Time* is my time to stand before the King of Kings. Think about our etiquette in the presence of a King. We bow down in reverence to honor him. When we come before the Lord, this should be our same posture—not asking for anything. Romans 12:1 (NIV) states, "Therefore, I urge you, brothers and sisters, in view of God's mercy, to offer your bodies as a living sacrifice, holy and pleasing to God—this is your true and proper worship."

God is not looking for you to be perfect and without flaws, because He knows you are still human, made of flesh. That's why we must pray daily, "Create in me a pure heart, O God, and renew a steadfast spirit within me" (Psalms 51:10 NIV).

As my Pastor always says, "Come as you are, but you won't stay as you are." Being with God is like going to school. We start off in kindergarten and eventually graduate from high school and some continue to college. It's a constant and consistent process. That's why our *Face Time* must be consistent because we grow as we advance to each new level of our lives, and our final accomplishment will be when He says, "Well done, my good and faithful servant. Enter into the glory of the Lord."

I am not perfect. I have traveled off course so many times, but because of God's grace, I am able to write this book and encourage you to keep it moving and don't give up on the call God has on your life.

If you still have breath in your body, you still have a chance to make a change. God is not looking for perfect people. In fact, he has no tolerance for the self -righteous. Sometimes people act like they were saved and had a relationship with God from the wound. God is looking for a pure heart. Not a religious fanatic.

If you could see what God has planned for your life you would keep pressing. Believe me he wants you to have his best and not settle for less. When you spend time with him daily he will give you clear instructions for your life. There is a lot of noise in the world, and sometimes it can be very loud, but we must listen to the voice of God. It can save you from so many years of heartache and stress.

Like me, you too may face spiritual and physical attacks, and during those lonely and painful moments, the only weapons of defense that you will have are the Word that you've stored in your heart and the faith you've built within your soul. Be diligent and dedicated about spending intimate time with the Lord. I pray that *Face Time* has been a blessing to you.

About the Author

After a near death experience last year, Alisa had her own personal encounter with God, which compelled her to share her *Face Time* up close experience with others. Alisa's passion is to address the spiritual and emotional needs of woman/men from all walks of life, those who have experienced self- esteem attacks, destiny attacks, spiritual attacks, experienced the effects of a divorce, being a single mom, recovering from bankruptcy, ups and downs of climbing the corporate ladder and becoming an entrepreneur, to bouncing back and taking control of her life and becoming a published author, coach, mentor, owning her own business, and soon releasing her first single music project.

Alisa notes we all share the same blood-line, but only a Face Time Encounter can give you direct access to the unlimited potential you each have inside of you.

Personal Information

Alisa is a loving mother of only child Ashley Marie; she has 3 beautiful grandchildren Jordyn, Jeremiah, and Aaliyah. Her parents encouraged her to further her education. Alisa graduated Magna Cum Laude with a BS in Business Administration/HR Management. She was born in Cleveland, Ohio. Alisa currently resides in the suburbs of Cuyahoga County, Ohio. Her personal interests include traveling, singing, writing, training, coaching and decorating. Alisa enjoys going to comedy shows, jazz clubs, going to sporting events, amusement parks, and she's a big movie buff.

Alisa's home church is The Word Church in Warrensville Heights, OH, where she has served in the Praise & Worship team for many years ministering at all 4 locations, serving under the leadership of Dr. R A Vernon & Lady Victory Vernon. Her passion is to motivate and push others into their destiny. Alisa has experienced many ups and downs in her life, but she never quit no matter what.

Current Business or Profession: International Best Selling Author, Motivational Speaker, Coach and Financial Advisor

Professional Background: Alisa has worked in Financial Services 28 yrs. (Banking, Advertising firm, Institutional Trading, HR) she is currently a Financial Advisor with Prudential. She has taught Financial Wellness classes such as Budgeting, Credit Enhancement and Identity Theft.

Education: Graduated Magna Cum Laude from Baker College in MI with her BA Business Admin/HR Management. She also has an AA in Business Administration from Cuyahoga Community College Eastern Campus, She's a Registered IAR (Investment Advisor), has her Life & Health license and Series 6 for the State of OH, TX and NY.

Previous Publishing Experience: No previous experience. This is her 1st book as an author (non-fiction)

Achievements & Awards: Alisa has written several Financial Articles for the Phenomenal Woman Magazine. Alisa was featured in Cuyahoga Community College's Job for Joy TV Commercial. She sung on the Bobby Jones Gospel Show in 1996 and she placed as a finalist in a talent contest, where she had the opportunity to sing at the MGM Grand Hotel in Las Vegas in 2007.

Major Influences in my Spiritual Growth: Alisa's Grandfather Lewis Riley, her dad Emanuel Riley, Dr. RA Vernon, Senior Pastor The Word Church, TD Jakes, John Gray, Bishop Eric K. Clark, Drs. Darrell & Belinda Scott, Joyce Meyer, Toure' Roberts, COGIC, countless mentors, pastors, worship leaders and friends who are responsible for helping her stay focused.

Contact Information

Email: authoralisatyler@gmail.com

Instagram: authoralisatyler

Facebook: Alisa Tyler

Website: www.alisatyler.com

To book Alisa Tyler for speaking engagements or coaching sessions visit www.alisatyler.com

We hope you enjoyed this heartfelt book exclusively distributed through Heart Centered Women Publishing™. If you're interested in getting information on Heart Centered Women Publishing™ products and services, please contact us:

Heart Centered Women Publishing™

Heart Centered Women Media™

Heart Centered Women TV™

Phone: (843) 376-9044

Website: www.heartcenteredwomenpublishing.com

Published and distributed in the United States by: Heart Centered Women Publishing™ www.heartcenteredwomenpublishing.com

Published and distributed Internationally by: Heart Centered Women Publishing™ www.heartcenteredwomenpublishing.com

<u>Start Living the Life You Dream</u>

Visit our talk radio show website www.successandbeautyradio.com and discover the most inspiring and successful beauty, business and lifestyle experts and entrepreneur's exclusive interviews including #1 International Best Selling Alisa Tyler!